**Improve Your Decision Making Skills**

# Improve Your Decision Making Skills

## Tom Philp

**McGRAW-HILL Book Company (UK) Limited**

**London** · New York · St Louis · San Francisco · Auckland
Bogotá · Guatemala · Hamburg · Johannesburg · Lisbon · Madrid
Mexico · Montreal · New Delhi · Panama · Paris · San Juan
São Paulo · Singapore · Sydney · Tokyo · Toronto

Published by
## McGRAW-HILL Book Company (UK) Limited
MAIDENHEAD · BERKSHIRE · ENGLAND

**British Library Cataloguing in Publication Data**

Philp, Tom
  Improve your decision making skills.
  1. Decision making
  I. Title
  658.4'03    HD30.23

ISBN 0-07-084766-5


**Library of Congress Cataloging in Publication Data**

Philp, Tom.
  Improve your decision making skills.

  Includes index.
  1. Decision making.    2. Middle managers—Decision making.   I. Title.
HD30.23.P49   1985      658.4'03     85-43
ISBN 0-07-084766-5




Copyright © 1985 McGraw-Hill Book Company (UK) Limited. All rights reserved. No part of this publication may be reproduced, stored in a retrieval system, or transmitted, in any form or by any means, electronic, mechanical, photocopying, recording, or otherwise, without the prior permission of McGraw-Hill Book Company (UK) Limited, or of the original copyright holder.

2345 WL 8876

Typeset by Eta Services (Typesetters) Ltd., Beccles, Suffolk.
Printed and Bound in Great Britain by
Whitstable Litho Ltd., Whitstable, Kent

# Contents

Preface      vii

Chapter 1    **The need to improve**    1
The problems encountered by organizations large and small would be reduced dramatically if greater attention to detail were given *before* decisions were made. Being decisive is only good when it is combined with the skill of making good decisions.

Chapter 2    **Clarifying the objective**    13
The importance of this very essential step in decision making is very often overlooked. Yet, if you don't know where you are going, any route will get you there! This chapter provides guidance on how to ensure that effort put into decision making is working towards the correct goal.

Chapter 3    **Consider the factors which will influence your choice of action**    35
This chapter deals with the means of collecting the information which will have to be used when comparing options open to you for the achievement of your stated objective.

Chapter 4    **Generating options**    47
An unbiased group of options is rarely found easily, but if the eventual choice is important, then the list of options to choose from must be the best possible.

# CONTENTS

**Chapter 5** **Comparing the options and making the choice**     55
Objective comparison of the options available is crucial if you are going to be prepared to live with your choice of action. Benefits of each option must be looked at in conjunction with risks involved. When a compromise has to be made, it must be the best available compromise from all aspects and viewpoints

**Chapter 6** **Presenting the recommendation**     71
Very seldom does the person who handles the decision have the ultimate authority to go ahead without agreement from some others. Good decisions can stand or fall at this stage.

**Chapter 7** **Planning for implementation**     79
This is action which is necessary if the good decision is to become an effective decision.

**Chapter 8** **Making it happen for you**     83
This chapter is designed to help you put into practice the skills of decision making to a decision of your own choice.

**Index**     97

# Preface

Why is it assumed so often that a person can be put into a managerial position, where so many decisions have to be made with serious repercussions if they go wrong, without adequate training in decision making?

Apart from the innocent belief that anyone can make decisions there would appear to be two distinct reasons for this folly.

One is the conviction that the ability to make decisions is a quality the person either possesses or does not, and therefore it cannot be trained into the person. This is a confusion between decisiveness and being able to make *good* decisions.

The other can be much more difficult to comprehend. Quite frankly, some people do not seem to realize what decisions are! While I was having a conversation with a personnel manager on one occasion, he explained to me that he had to choose an organization to come into his company to carry out some decision making training. He was asking for my views on how I would carry out such training. I mentioned that the training should be totally related to their needs and that anyone who attended a course should bring with them a decision they were currently working on. We could then use these decisions to teach the process and they would see real benefit from the results.

The personnel manager informed me that the managers in his company did not really make decisions—in fact he could use himself as an example because he did not get involved with making decisions either. (Who made the decision to bring someone in to teach decision making?)

I politely suggested to him that if he had been trained in decision making, he would have found making the choice of an organization to come in to train the managers an easier *decision* to handle. Also, he was surely involved with the selection of people, and possibly their dismissal—only two other examples of significant decisions which have to be handled properly.

Managers at all levels *are* involved with numerous important decisions: purchasing, selling, designing, manufacturing, supervising, budgeting, and many, many more. It is essential that the skills involved with making decisions improve.

Put effort into your own improvement and you will reap the benefits that are there for you, and for the people who work for you.

**Acknowledgement**

*My thanks to my wife Barbara, my family and friends, for their help and tolerance*

# 1.

# The need to improve

The increasing complexity of business and of industrial relations highlights the need for improvement in the underlying thinking behind decision making in organizations of all sizes, and at all levels within these organizations. All too often when a situation is getting out of control a cry can be heard, 'I wish we'd thought of that before we went ahead,' or possibly a louder cry of 'Surely they realized that would happen.' Examples are numerous and they can be seen daily. Is it any wonder that the people who are affected by the result of decisions made by others are demanding more and more consultation?

A rather extreme example of the need to improve was seen a few years ago in a small engineering company run by an entrepreneur. A recession had been forecast so he knew he had to have a tighter control of his costs. The decision made was to cut out all non-essential services and he stated these to be advertising and sales, training, and research and development.

In reality these investment areas are the life-blood of successful companies and as such are essential services; money spent on advertising and sales will increase the opportunities to sell the product; investment in good training will increase the chances of improving production of the product and the management of the business; research and development will allow the company to stay ahead of the competition by the introduction of improved products and new ideas.

In the case of this small engineering company, was it the recession which caused the company to lose business and make people redundant, or was it more likely the owner's ineptness at handling decisions?

The above example may seem to be a very obvious mistake to make, but what about the less obvious oversight?

A large hotel group decided on a course of action aimed at encouraging new business by offering certain incentives to new customers. For example, a number of nights spent in any of their hotels would qualify you for a weekend stay. A regular user of this hotel group was delighted with the idea until he was informed that as a high volume customer he could not take part in the scheme. The reason given for the exclusion was that this customer was on reduced rates because of the high volume of business he brought to the hotel and it was unreasonable for anyone on reduced rates to expect to take part in the new business campaign. The customer in question was not too pleased at first, but soon realized that the solution was simple. All he had to do was to give the majority of his business to another hotel group, which would also give him reduced rates, and he would then be able to qualify for the free weekends from the original hotel group by virtue of his reduced business with them.

Someone, somewhere, was responsible for handling the decision on the new business campaign, but is it unreasonable to expect that they should have considered what their chosen action could do to existing customers? Many people still make decisions on the basis of what the decision will do for them and ignore what it may do *to* them. But, of course, if trade does fall as a result of a decision like the one in this hotel example, it is easy to find a scapegoat in the form of the difficulty of getting good staff, or there is always the recession to fall back on if you are really stuck. By chance, as I was putting some thoughts on paper for this book, I overheard another hotel example. I was sitting in a quiet corner of the lounge in an hotel—not one from the group in the previous example—when the bar manager came in to advise the young lady behind the bar that bar snacks were going up in price 'as from today'.

It turned out the increases were going to double the price of sandwiches and snacks. The young lady said, 'But no one will buy them at that price.' His reply was: 'I can't help that, I've got to get my bottom line profit figure correct.' I resisted the temptation to question if there were not other options worth considering, rather than the extreme price increases.

Making decisions without adequate thought occurs all too frequently. In fact it appears to be positively encouraged by some people. The following quotation is taken from an article on decision making which appeared in a well-known management magazine:

> When I was a young man in business, I was taught that when making decisions, I had to think them through, look at options, consider the risks and the benefits, and make a careful choice. However, now that the recession is causing so many economic difficulties, I realize that there is not

time for such refinements and decisions have to be made boldly.

This attitude towards decision making is responsible for most of the problems industry and commerce are faced with. Take, for example, the problems which a well-known manufacturer of consumer products was faced with: a serious decline in cooperation between manufacturing and sales and an increase in complaints from customers about late and sometimes no deliveries.

Some months previously the sales director decided he could take 15 per cent of the market away from the major competitor by increasing his sales promotions. Extra prizes were given to sales people who could obtain new business, and incentives were given to distributors for extra orders given.

Within three months of the introduction of the sales campaign, an increase of $12\frac{1}{2}$ per cent in orders received by the company proved the sales director to be correct in his judgement.

Unfortunately the company's manufacturing capability for these products was already stretched at 100 per cent capacity before the campaign was launched, and it would cost £5.5 million to increase capacity to cope with the increased orders. Neither space nor money was available for such an increase. This was information which the sales director could have found out previously had he taken the trouble to think about what he was doing, rather than apparently following the advice given in the previous quotation.

Fortunately for the people employed, and for the company as a whole, the managing director and the sales director did not follow through with their decision (made over lunch) to resolve the situation by completely rearranging the factory and resiting the manufacture of the problem products some 35 miles away.

Managers like these very seldom have space problems for long. When I last heard of them they were looking for ways to recover some of the customers they had lost—they have the space to do it because of the lost business. Let's hope this time they are taking the time and using the skills that are required for good decisions to be made.

A possible reason for so many dreadful decisions is confusion between decisiveness and good decision making.

**Decisiveness** is defined as influential, conclusive, and characterized by the ability to make quick decisions.
**Decision** is defined as judgement, resolution, and purpose.

What some people seem to expect is decisiveness, without realizing that the skill in making decisions does take time. The time needed will depend on the seriousness of the decision to be made.

An interview reported in a well-known international newspaper where a journalist was interviewing Prime Minister Margaret Thatcher seems to confirm this opinion. One of the questions put to Mrs Thatcher included the following: 'But are you so resolute? When you face awkward decisions like whether to hold a general election, you dither like most of us don't you?'

I can recall a manager in a large manufacturing company who did not like people to dither. He certainly did not dither himself when he was faced with managerial decisions—he was decisive. For example, during the three-day working week in the UK in 1974, when there were restrictions on how much electricity factories could draw from the mains supply, one of his managers approached him at the end of their third day's production with the message that by hiring some generators they could make their own electricity the next day, thereby keeping production going past the three days.

'Good,' said our decisive manager, 'let's bring our workforce in tomorrow.' The message he received the next morning was quite different: it had not been possible to hire the generators. The decisive manager's reply this time, roughly translated, was 'Oh dear, we'll have to send the workforce home.' The repercussions which followed those two quick (and too quick) decisions took a long time to die down. Would it have been dithering to consider the certainty or otherwise of his information, and what action he could take if it turned out to be invalid, **before** being so decisive?

Strangely enough, the people who advocate decisiveness and say that any decision is better than no decision very rarely apply the same logic to their domestic life where their own money and feelings are at risk.

Surely we've all seen people take more time over a choice from a menu than they would take to make many of their decisions at work. The truth of this was brought home to me in a hotel restaurant when I could not avoid overhearing the conversation at the next table. A group of managers were discussing decision making and one of them said, 'I like people who are decisive—right or wrong, at least they make a decision.' Yes, he was the one that the waitress had to visit three times to find out what he wanted—he could not make up his mind. Sadly, I doubt if he recognized the connection.

We do make some very significant decisions in our domestic life: what job to do, where to work, who to work for, whether to get married or stay single, who to marry, which

## THE NEED TO IMPROVE

car to buy, or which house to buy or rent. These decisions take time and we will make the time available to us. Could you possibly imagine a conversation at home that went like this ... 'Yes, I know that the house I've bought is too small, and it does not have enough bedrooms but I was being pushed by the estate agent for an answer and I like to be decisive.' It may appear frivolous to compare domestic examples with work decisions, because time pressure is normally not so great in the domestic situation. However, it does prove that more care is taken when we truly have to live with the outcome of our decisions. This book will show you how to apply the same care to your business decisions which will allow you to be justly proud to live with them.

The intention is not to ignore the pressures of work, or the difficulties time pressure brings, but the lack of time to make a decision is not a good reason for making a lot of wrong decisions. A decision to delay making a choice of action could be the most appropriate thing to do on occasions—but it still has to be thought through.

There may never seem to be time to do things properly, but is there time to do them again? Having to do things again, or spending time trying to repair the damage caused, can result in industrial unrest, lost profits, poor cash flow, high rejects, customer dissatisfaction, or lost sales—to name but a few.

Decision making is like dropping a pebble into a pond: it will make ripples. Consideration has to be given to the likely size of the ripples *before* you drop the pebble. Trying to remove the pebble with your hand will not stop the ripples —it's more likely to make them bigger.

To develop the care that is needed in decision making

requires us simply to apply a very straightforward logical set of principles, or as I prefer to see them, steps on a stairway. It becomes more difficult to climb the stairs to get where you want to, if you choose to miss out some of the steps.

### Step 1   Clarify your objective

This first step in decision making should be the most obvious of all, and yet its importance is very often overlooked. Surely it is essential that before we do anything we should be clear in our minds what it is that we need to achieve, or what the situation should look like when our decision is implemented.

The companies in the first two examples described in this chapter would not have suffered the results experienced if someone had clarified the precise objective the company wanted to achieve. I'm sure neither of the companies wanted to lose business.

### Step 2   Consider the factors which will influence your choice of action

This step provides for the collection of information which will be used when comparing the options open to you for the achievement of your stated objective. It will be very difficult to make a genuine comparison regarding the risks and benefits associated with each of the options if there is not a clear understanding of the results required, the resources available, constraints which exist, and any possible implication which could follow.

It is this step which will reduce the chances of having to say, 'I wish we'd thought about that before we went ahead.'

## Step 3  Generating options

Dependent upon the type of decision in hand, the search for methods of accomplishing the overall objective will vary in difficulty. For example the choice of equipment or choice of person to fill a particular vacancy, or the choice of location of a new department or factory will require the effective use of all relevant sources of information to identify where options may exist. In some instances, like the development of new approaches to situations, it may be appropriate to use the 'brainstorming' technique. Many good new ideas can result from this when it is conducted properly. Additionally, special techniques to overcome any possible personal prejudice will work towards an unbiased list of options being developed.

To complete the list, don't forget to include the option to do nothing. The status quo in some cases can end up as the best option.

## Step 4  Comparing the options and making the choice

A comparison of each option against the previously agreed factors can now be made. This will show how well each option satisfies or otherwise the areas that were declared to be important. Should an option fail to satisfy a factor which you determined to be absolutely crucial, then that option can be eliminated straight away.

This will leave the time available to be spent most efficiently and effectively comparing only those options which match your declared limits. Repeating something which has been said earlier, do avoid the temptation to look at an option with regard to only what it can do for you, without realizing what it could do to you. As this is the last chance to look at the options before commitment is made, a little constructive pessimism can be useful. A look into the future to compare benefits with possible in-built risks will allow the best-balanced choice to be made. This is when you can be decisive —with confidence.

### Step 5   Presenting the recommendation

Unless the decision is entirely your responsibility, you will have to convince someone else to agree before action can be taken. A decision well thought through is an easier decision to recommend than one which is based only on the feeling that it is right. However, many decisions fail to get approval to go ahead due to the manner in which the recommendation is passed to the person, or persons, who eventually have the final word.

While you must determine the most appropriate method of presenting your recommendation, whether this be formally or informally, in written form or by word of mouth, the rules are similar and must be followed if you want success in getting your recommendation accepted.

### Step 6   Plan for implementation

Seeing well thought through decisions, which have been accepted in principle, collecting dust on the shelves of

## THE NEED TO IMPROVE

managers because no-one is doing anything about implementing the recommendation shows a dreadful waste of time, effort and money.

Planning for implementation is essential if we are to ensure that the good decision becomes an effective decision. This will vary, dependent on the kind of decision being handled, from a short checklist of things done to an extensive planning chart where the coordination of several other people is required. Whichever method is chosen the elements are common, and care must be taken to ensure that potential snags identified are well catered for in the plan.

Until we improve the way decisions are handled we cannot expect others to have confidence in our decisions. It is only

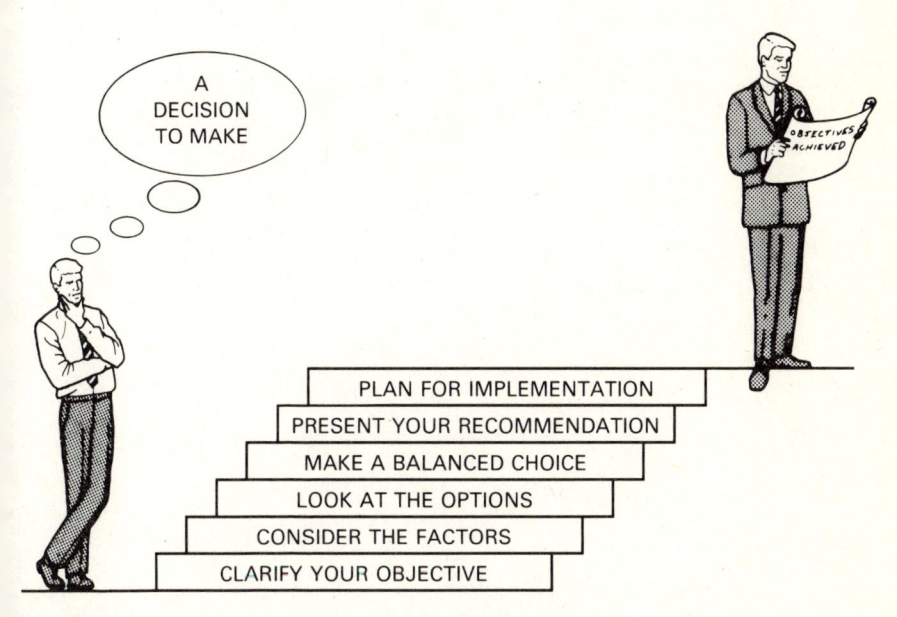

**Figure 1.1** The steps for good decision making

when that confidence is earned that we can have more justifiable confidence in ourselves. This will allow us to prosper as managers, and our companies can be more assured of continued success and progress.

# 2.

# Clarifying the objective

The first step towards an effective decision has to be a clear statement of the precise objective to be achieved; without this, a number of new difficulties can be created. This may seem to be an outstandingly obvious statement to make but it never fails to amaze me how often the importance of taking the time to establish precisely what it is that has to be achieved is overlooked.

While I was visiting a company recently, one of the managers outlined to me a typical example. The company was housed in a three-storey building, and for very good reasons the third floor was selected to be used as a laboratory where a team of engineers worked on new product research and development. On occasions the engineers required a special kind of gas for their experiments but there was no problem because it was readily available from a local supplier. Orders were placed for the gas to be delivered on demand, as and when it was needed. The requirement was not excessive so it was decided that the standard size of container would suffice. To comply with safety regulations the company built a storage area for the gas containers and this was located as close to the engineers as was permitted by law.

Each time a new supply of gas was delivered, someone had the unenviable task of carrying the heavy replacement containers up three flights of stairs and carrying the empty ones down again. As there was no lift in the building, many attempts were made to simplify the task of transporting the containers up and down the stairs. The latest idea had been the purchase of a specially designed trolley which by its wheel design could be used on stairways. This was found to be the best solution to date, but it was not considered to be very practical or safe.

Fortunately it did not take the company too long to realize that their efforts had not been channelled towards the correct objective: it was the gas they required on the third floor, not necessarily the containers.

By tackling their more precise objective, which was to establish the best way to supply gas to the engineers, they were able to resolve the situation more simply by piping gas up from a ground-floor storage area.

So you see, the statement of your precise objective not only keeps you on track, but it also opens up options which may have been overlooked—as a sales manager found out in a not uncommon situation.

The sales manager was concerned that his sales force were not fully up to date with regard to technical knowledge of the products they were selling. He believed that they would be more able to handle certain situations if they were more conversant with manufacturing problems. The decision the sales manager reached was to send each of his seven sales people into the factory on a rota basis, to spend two weeks touring the five main manufacturing areas. Needless to say, the manager's sales director was not happy to support a decision

## CLARIFYING THE OBJECTIVE

which would mean taking 70 man days away from the selling role.

To ease the sales manager's frustration at not being able to implement his decision, I asked him to tell me what his objective was. He said that he wanted to increase product knowledge and awareness of manufacturing problems in his sales team. This, of course, is far too vague. What specific knowledge? What specific problems? And to what extent will these vary between sales people? It is only when the sales manager has the answers to these questions that he should be thinking about how to establish the best way to provide the information.

The sales manager in the situation actually had three separate tasks to work on:

– He needed to establish clearly what information the sales people should be aware of.
– He needed to find out the extent of this knowledge with regard to each individual in the team.
– He needed to determine the best methods to provide the information.

When it was established clearly what information the sales people should have, a simple checklist of questions was sent to each member of the sales team and, depending on the quality of the answers received back, action was taken to fill the appropriate gaps.

The methods used to provide answers varied from a telephone call into the factory to a two-day instructional tour of some of the departments. No more than nine man days were taken out from the selling role, which was considerably less than the estimated 70.

There is a common factor when we look at the difficulty some people experience when trying to be clear with regard to their objective. This is a confusion between **what they want to do** with **what they need to achieve**. Mostly people focus on the former.

The example which still occurs often is when someone decides to send a member of their team on a training course. I recall a manager asking if I knew of any training courses his secretary could attend. Of course, the answer had to be, 'Yes, there are many.' When I probed to identify a part of her job where training could help her develop, he informed me that she was perfect. What he wanted was to send her on a course as a reward for her efforts because she would have noticed that her colleagues had been away on courses and she hadn't.

I suggested he spoke to the lady to find out how she felt about the job to see if there were areas where she could do with some help, but I felt like suggesting he send her on a one-week holiday at the coast with all expenses paid.

However, it is not always this easy to separate what you want to do from what has to be achieved. While I was working with another sales manager he explained to me that an objective he had been working on for some time without success was 'how to recruit a sales person for the London area'. I asked if he did not really mean, 'Which sales person do I recruit for the London area?' His response was, 'I wish I had a choice.'

It transpired that the company was based many miles from the London area, and all employees were regarded as being located at the head office irrespective of where they worked. The manager's difficulty, therefore, was getting someone to

## CLARIFYING THE OBJECTIVE

sell in London while he was unable to pay that person London rates.

After further discussion on the subject we resolved that the manager's objective should really be stated as 'finding the best method for obtaining sales in the London area', which would allow us to look at employing a sales person as only one of the options.

As a matter of interest, the situation was resolved soon after by approaching a company which was selling products which were complementary to this company's product range. They made that company an agent to sell for them and the redefined objective was achieved.

As can be seen from the above example, there is no precise formula which can be used to clarify your objective. It requires time and self-discipline, and depends on your willingness to question what you originally believed to be your goal. The following guidelines are simply an aid, to help you to be sure you are starting off in the correct direction.

### Guidelines for clarifying your objective

- Look at the complete situation and determine precisely what it is that has to be achieved, corrected, maintained, improved, or created. This is sometimes phrased: 'If only we could get this done, most of our difficulties would be resolved.'
- Write out what you believe your objective to be—any difficulty in succinctly stating your objective is sometimes an indication that you are not entirely clear.

- Study the written objective, and question if it is specific enough with regard to what has to be arrived at. For example, you may have stated 'improve profitability', which is rather vague. Do you not know what is hindering profitability? If it is an overrun on costs on a particular product, it may be better for you to work on an objective which is geared to finding the best way to reduce those specific costs. The more specific we can be at this stage, the less time will be needed to arrive at a good decision.

- Scrutinize the written objective to ensure that you have not made decisions within your statement of objective without realizing it. For example, a question which asks, 'Which new machine do I buy?' automatically rules out second-hand machines and also rental or leasing. This may be a correct thing to do, but there has to be conscious recognition of those built-in decisions if we are to proceed with confidence.

- Always ensure that you are focusing on what has to be arrived at, rather than what you want to do.

- Phrasing your objective as a question whenever possible helps you to stay on track throughout the rest of the decision making process—for example, 'What is the best way to . . . ?' constantly serves as a reminder of what it is you are aiming at.

- Throughout the task of clarifying your objective, don't be afraid to use the question 'Why?'

A clear objective provides an excellent base for a logical progression to an effectively implemented decision; therefore time spent at this stage of decision making will provide a real

## CLARIFYING THE OBJECTIVE

return on the investment. Practise your skills on the following case studies.

## A case study on clarifying the objective

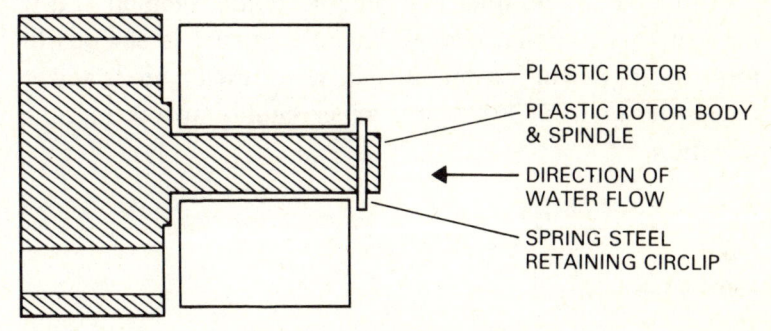

Figure 2.1  Cross-sectional view of a standard 1½-inch water meter.

THE SITUATION

The company has been manufacturing and selling meters for measuring the flow of water for many years. The 1½-inch model is the best-seller and is exported to over 60 countries. The meter in its standard design as shown above is acceptable to most countries in the world, but because of the condition of the water in one particular country, it insists that the meter is supplied with a stainless steel circlip in place of the standard spring steel, to prevent corrosion.

THE PROBLEM

Stainless steel circlips are much more expensive to purchase than the standard spring steel, but as sales to the country represent 12 per cent of the total sales of the 1½-inch meter, the request is honoured.

Buying, pricing, manufacturing, assembly, quality control, storing and marketing two assemblies with only a slight difference causes problems, as well as being far from economical.

Although the product is profitable at the moment and it performs its function very well, the company is anxious to improve its overall profitability in water meter sales, and it recognizes that this is one area which could improve its contribution.

YOUR TASK

Assume yourself to be a member of the design and development department. You have been asked to examine the $1\frac{1}{2}$-inch water meter situation and decide how it can be improved. You know, of course, that your first step in decision making is a clear statement of your objective.

It is this step only that you are going to concentrate on because you know if you get your objective correct, the rest of the decision making effort will be efficiently and effectively utilized. How would you phrase your objective?

Sample statements of objectives are shown on the following page. Compare yours to see how you performed.

THE WATER METER CASE STUDY SAMPLE OBJECTIVES

| Statement of objective | Author's comment |
|---|---|
| Improve profitability. | No one can argue, but is it not rather too vague? |

## CLARIFYING THE OBJECTIVE

| *Statement of objective* | *Author's comment* |
|---|---|
| Find a suitable material for a circlip which will be acceptable to all countries. | Why constrain yourself to only one way to retain the rotor on the spindle? |
| Establish an assembly which is acceptable to all countries. | On the right track, no doubt, but could it not be expressed more precisely? |
| Establish the best* way to retain the rotor on the spindle. | †A precise statement of what needs to be achieved. |

Working towards the objective 'to establish the best way to retain the rotor on the spindle' allows for more options to be generated. When comparisons are made, the circlip will have its chance to prove itself against the factors chosen.

In the actual case this study was taken from, the company arrived at a slight redesign of the spindle and rotor which did away with any need for a circlip at all.

The simplified design and the removal of the duplication in buying, pricing, manufacturing, assembling, quality control, storing and marketing, showed tremendous savings which enhanced the company's profitability considerably. This was something which was not available previously, as the engineers had been working on a different objective: 'to find a circlip with material suitable to all countries'—an example of a built-in decision which prevented the generation and consideration of other options.

---

\* The word 'best' will be described by the factors which will influence the choice of action—Step 2 in decision making

† As the circlip, in whichever material, just performs the function of retaining the rotor on the spindle, it can be said that a circlip is just one of the options open to you.

The water meter case was a relatively straightforward kind of decision to handle, although it does demonstrate the need to be careful when determining your objective. Some situations that managers find themselves in are a great deal more complex. The next case study is more typical of the latter.

I would like you to be able to refer back to this case on occasions in further chapters, so I will call the company the Decision Making Organization, or DM for short.

## The DM Organization case study

DM is a medium-sized company employing 400 people, manufacturing and marketing competitive quality office furniture.

The company started in the office furniture business approximately 45 years ago. It moved from the craftsman-built furniture employing nine skilled craftsmen, to mass production employing 150 people within its first 10 years. Further growth came about after securing several contracts to supply government offices.

Steady growth continued until about 10 years ago. Since then the present organization structure and the number of employees has remained fairly static. A full three-shift system in operation is working well.

The premises which are owned by the company are in a suitable area with easy access to road and rail services, and a good supply of labour. There is not a great deal of industry in the area, and certainly no competitor for the product range. DM is very proud of its reputation for good products and also for its good record for industrial relations.

# CLARIFYING THE OBJECTIVE

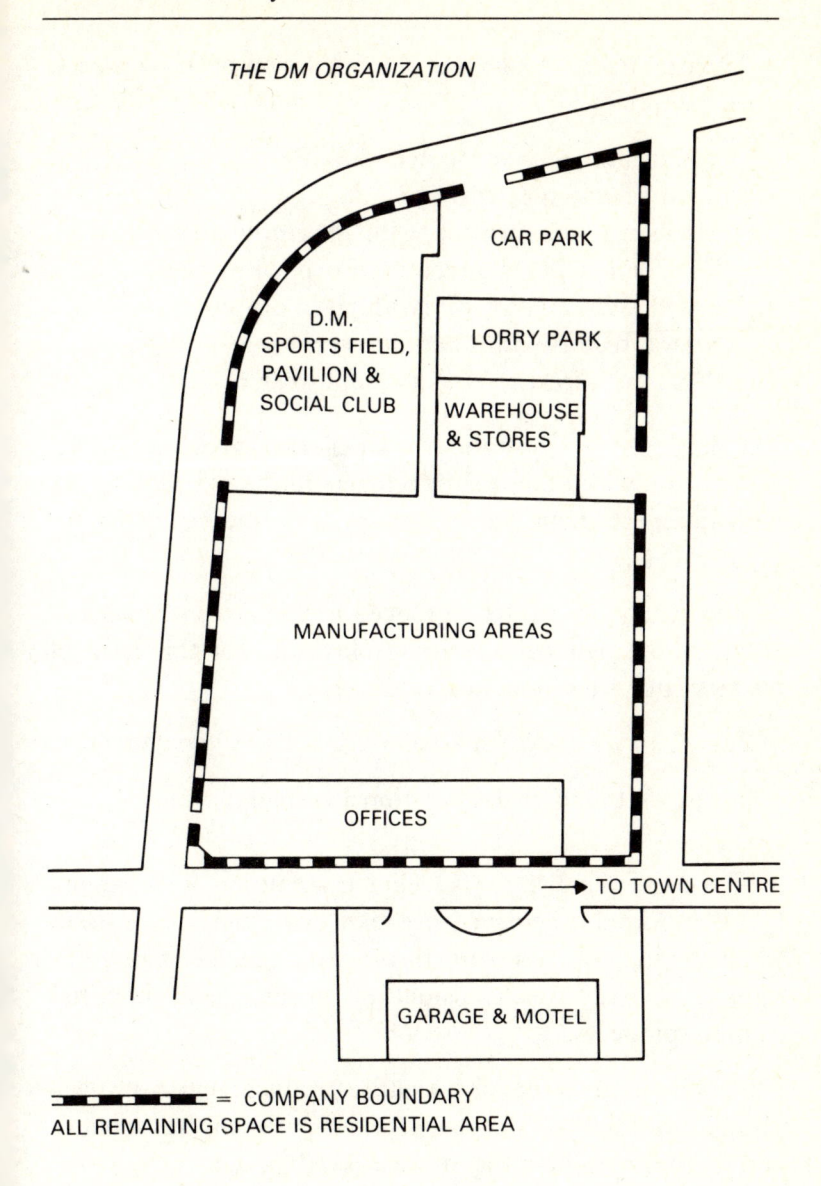

**Figure 2.2**  Layout of the DM Organization

## IMPROVE YOUR DECISION MAKING SKILLS

The characters involved in the discussion of the company are as follows:

The managing director with a staff of:
- Finance director (with 45 employees)
- Manufacturing director (with 234 employees)
- Plant and facilities director (with 45 employees)
- Product design director (with 30 employees)
- Sales director (with 24 employees)
- Personnel director (with 15 employees)

The net profit to sales ratio is 7.5 per cent, which is low but comparable with other manufacturers in the office furniture trade (a reflection on the very competitive trading conditions in the industry).

The return on capital employed is 11 per cent, which is ahead of the national average profitability for this kind of business and is considered acceptable.

Raw material stocks turn over once in every 200 days.

Debtors settle in 70 days (national average).

The managing director is feeling quite proud of the results he has managed to achieve since taking over the MD position when joining the company three years ago. He has every right to feel satisfied, considering the problems inherited from his predecessor.

Sales have increased for the entire product range manufactured in the factory. The marketing department has actually said there is no sign of the increase levelling out.

Labour turnover has dropped to well below the average for the area. It is likely that a major reason for this is

# CLARIFYING THE OBJECTIVE

The following is the financial situation of the company based on the results of the past year.

*Profit statement*

| | £ |
|---|---|
| Sales | 5 424 000 |
| Net profit before tax | 406 000 |
| Taxation for the year | 205 000 |
| Profit after tax | 201 000 |

*Balance sheet*

| | | |
|---|---|---|
| Fixed assets | | |
|   Land and buildings | | 1 007 000 |
|   Plant and equipment | | 427 000 |
|   Motor vehicles | | 95 000 |
| | | 1 529 000 |
| Current assets | | |
|   Inventories | 2 160 000 | |
|   Debtors | 1 033 000 | |
|   Cash | 19 000 | |
| | 3 212 000 | |
| Creditors; amounts falling due within one year | | |
|   Creditors | 1 056 000 | |
|   Bank overdraft | 32 000 | |
| | 1 088 000 | |
| Net current assets | | 2 124 000 |
| Capital employed | | 3 653 000 |
| Creditors; amounts falling due after one year | | |
|   Loan stock | | 215 000 |
| Net assets less external finance | | 3 438 000 |
| Capital and reserves | | |
|   Share capital | | 1 726 000 |
|   Profit from prior years | | 1 511 000 |
|   Current profit | | 201 000 |
| Shareholders' interest | | £3 438 000 |

increased job security through the extensive demand for the products manufactured.

Reducing the number of small independent storage areas and consolidating them into one warehouse under the direct control of a warehouse and stores manager freed a considerable amount of space. There had been a real demand for space, particularly by the main assembly lines.

With manufacturing now running at full capacity, it is just as well that the machine maintenance programme introduced last year is working very well. Not much time is being lost by production breakdowns, although improvements are still being looked for.

In preparation for the board meeting scheduled for next month, the managing director has asked each of his directors for their up-to-date views on the situation in their departments. This information will help him to develop his plans for the future direction of the company. Their replies can be found on the following pages.

CLARIFYING THE OBJECTIVE

# Memorandum

**To** Managing Director

**From** Finance Director

          PLANNING FOR THE FUTURE

I believe that the next 12 months is critical and that we must establish clear priorities for this period.

The Chairman has made it clear that we must continue to increase our sales volume and market share. The main constraint is our inability to produce enough, despite modern and efficient equipment. There is a growing lead time for our products although we are working to present capacity.

Finance is not a bar to increasing capacity:
— the banks are prepared to give short-term credit of £1m for a maximum of 2 years
— we could obtain a 15-year loan of around £1.2m
— improved stock control could provide the working capital for the required increase.

# Memorandum

**To** Managing Director

**From** Manufacturing Director

             BOARD MEETING

May we please discuss the question of our future product range?

The number and variety of products are causing us problems in stock control, scheduling and, inevitably, quality control. This is a major contributor to our production difficulties and lengthening delivery position.

## Memorandum

**To** Managing Director

**From** Sales Director

As you know the overall picture is excellent — certainly the best for the last six years. Our market share has improved steadily, but over the past six months the increase has flattened from 2.5 per cent to 0.8 per cent.

Analysis of sales reports show consistent satisfaction with our products and prices but reveals a growing concern over our delivery times.

We need to increase our product range in order to optimize our supply position. We calculate that an extra 6 per cent of business on existing lines can be achieved thus, in addition to new product sales, but we must improve our delivery times in order to realize this exciting potential.

CLARIFYING THE OBJECTIVE

# Memorandum

**To** Managing Director

**From** Product Design Director

> BOARD MEETING ON FIVE YEAR PLAN

I would like to raise and discuss the following points:

1. <u>New Product Design</u>
   Marketing are confident this will be a market leader.
   a) because of superior quality
   b) because it will be very competitive in price
   c) because it will be the first on the market.

2. <u>Training on new product</u>
   a) operator training or retraining — methods
   b) operator training or retraining — timing
   c) operator training or retraining — location
   d) operator training or retraining — payment during training period.

3. <u>Incentive scheme for engineers</u>
   a) 10 per cent bonus payable after 12 months' sales for each engineer on the design team which initiates a market leader product
   b) this has been agreed in principle with personnel.

## Memorandum

**To** Managing Director

**From** Plant and Facilities Director

### FUTURE PLANS

The main area of concern in my department is our machine maintenance programme.

Because capacity is being fully utilized it is remarkable that we have been able to reduce machine down time for the second year running, but I am very concerned that we shall not be able to continue the improvement.

As you know, I believe strongly that the present shortage of space throughout the factory is a great threat to our efficient operation and I trust that we shall institute plans to overcome this.


## Memorandum

**To** Managing Director

**From** Personnel Director

### BOARD MEETING

The matters of principal interest to my department which I would like raised at the board meeting are:

CLARIFYING THE OBJECTIVE

1. <u>Safety</u>
Considerable and continual obstruction of gangways and exits by supplies to manufacturing lines. This is an increasing problem and contravenes the HSW Act, is in many cases a fire hazard and has caused a series of avoidable accidents.

2. <u>Staff Turnover</u>
While, as you are aware, our hourly-paid staff turnover has reduced to the lowest in comparable situations in this area, managerial turnover has increased by 14 per cent on last year. Exit interviews by departmental heads define the main cause as the apparent lack of prospects for advancement.

3. <u>Training</u>
The programme of training throughout all levels, which we developed since you joined us, has been successful in improving manufacturing times and quality and reducing labour turnover. In addition it has been possible to free the area previously used for operator training and this is earmarked for a rest area to ease the pressure on the canteen caused by shortage of space.

When you have fully digested the case study background and read through each of the replies to the managing director, we can look at the situation through the eyes of the MD, to define an objective which should be worked towards if he is to resolve the majority of the company's current and potential difficulties.

Should you wish to work on the case study on your own to the point of defining an objective, please do so. You will then be able to compare your thoughts with the notes on the pages that follow.

CLARIFYING THE DM ORGANIZATION OBJECTIVE

The guidelines suggest that we look at the complete situation to determine what has to be done to remove most of the difficulties.

We will start off, therefore, by listing the various difficulties as seen by the different directors.

*Finance director:*
— Inability to produce enough.
— Growing lead times.
— Working to full capacity.
— Raw material stock control.

*Manufacturing director:*
— Product range too wide.
— Raw material stock control.
— Scheduling.
— Quality control.
— Production difficulties.
— Delivery times.

*Sales director:*
— Market share.
— Delivery times.
— Need to increase product range.

*Design and development director:*
— Ready to launch new product.
— Needs operator training for new product.
— Is committed to new product by bonus agreement.

*Plant and facilities director:*
- Fully utilized machines outstripping maintenance programme.
- Shortage of space.

*Personnel director:*
- Gangways congested.
- Poor managerial prospects.
- Has had to take over operator training space to increase canteen space.

Although this is a long list of difficulties, there do appear to be one or two common threads:

- The market is there but we can't meet it.
- Delivery times are poor.
- Raw material stock control is bad.
- Pressure on manufacturing.
- New products available—no space to train new operators.
- A wide range of products—but the market seems to want them all.
- Difficulty in scheduling.
- Quality control is under pressure.
- Fully utilized machines are outstripping the maintenance programme.
- Shortage of space in general.
- Safety hazards.
- Poor prospects for management growth.

The raw material stock turnover situation should be looked at without question, but the difficulty which most people seem to be suffering from is space. If we were able to overcome the space difficulty it would resolve the majority of the other difficulties experienced. Whereas if the raw

## IMPROVE YOUR DECISION MAKING SKILLS

material stock control system was looked at first, it is doubtful if it would impact as greatly.

We can test space out against the shortened list above. If we overcome the space problem:

- We would have a better chance of meeting the market needs.
- We could improve our delivery time.
- We would relieve the pressure on manufacturing.
- We would be able to train new operators on the new products.
- We could then give the market the new products it wants.
- We might reduce the difficulty in scheduling.
- We may take some pressure away from quality control.
- We could take the pressure away from maintenance.
- We would reduce safety hazards.
- There may be better prospects for managers.

You may be concerned that the results to be gained if space is resolved are not stated positively enough. All we are doing at this stage is to define our objective. The quality of the results will depend on the way we handle the remaining steps in the decision making process.

Should we agree that it is space which has to be tackled as the major contributing factor, the objective can be written thus:

What is the best way to overcome the space problem?

Testing this against the guidelines set out previously seems to confirm that we can confidently proceed towards a resolution.

This case study will continue to be used as a working example in the following chapters.

# 3.

# Consider the factors which will influence your choice of action

There are all too many instances where people have underestimated the need for this second step in decision making. And yet, as stated previously, it is the step which will reduce the chances of having to admit that you had overlooked something of significant value, which is quite easy to do under pressure.

An amusing little example of this came to my attention some years ago, where a man was very proudly showing a colleague of his around a newly built factory which was just ready for the grand opening. The colleague had noticed little grey boxes on the walls of each department they went through. The boxes were fitted some six feet from the floor and just out of reach for the rather short person being shown around. The boxes had not been mentioned during the tour so the visitor enquired as to their purpose. He was duly informed that the little grey boxes were the new electronic clocking stations where employees placed their clock cards before starting work. As the visitor struggled to reach one of the boxes he asked why they had been fitted so high on the walls. The reason given was to the effect that if the boxes were lower on the walls some of the employees would put orange peel and cigarette packets in them—he knew that from previous experience. Placing the boxes high on the wall would prevent that happening. 'How do rather short people like me reach to put their clock card in?' enquired the visitor. 'Oh dear, we forgot about that,' came the reply.

Even when more serious consequences can result, some people don't seem to think before they decide.

A well-known manufacturer of commercial vehicles was due to bring on to the market their latest improved design of traction unit for pulling larger improved trailers. As the company would actually be using some of the new vehicles for its own delivery of parts and accessories, a number of the newly designed trailers were ordered for the company's own use. The new trailers were delivered on schedule, smartly painted in the company's colours and with the company's name emblazoned as a travelling advert for their automotive products. Unfortunately, the manufacture of their own traction units had suffered a two-month delay. In order that the new trailers could be used for the improved deliveries they were purchased for, the company purchased a number of traction units from its major competitor to cover the two-month period until their own vehicles would be ready. When asked if the company had considered the possible impact on their own customers and potential customers, seeing the company's product being transported by a competitor's vehicles, the reply was 'We hadn't thought of that.'

I am often reminded that it is not always possible to cover everything, and I must concede this, but what about the following example.

## FACTORS WHICH WILL INFLUENCE YOUR CHOICE OF ACTION

A manufacturing company was faced with a decline in the demand for its products. The fall in orders was mainly due to a change in technology. There was little the company could do about that but what had to be done was to make adjustments in order to manufacture to meet the reduced demand as effectively and efficiently as possible.

Two separate manufacturing units were no longer viable and it was decided that the factory 400 miles from the main location would have to close down. Anyone currently working in the factory which was due to close down would be offered employment and resettlement assistance should they wish to transfer to the establishment which was to stay open. Others would be treated as fairly as possible with regard to redundancy payments. Three months after the completion of the closure of the factory and the transfer of some of the employees, a very difficult industrial relations situation developed. The company had apparently overlooked the fact that a difference in wages of 10 per cent gave no real problems when the people were separated by 400 miles, but now that they were on the same location there were demands—some for parity, others for retention of the differential.

The above example, however ludicrous, is in no way unique. Only recently while working in a very well known international company, one of the managers explained to me a problem he was experiencing. His own manager had suggested that his 'powers of leadership' were suspect. He was in charge of 14 people in an order processing department, and he was having difficulty building team spirit. This was defined in the following terms: poor morale, lack of cooperation between team members, no one willing to back up or help out another member of the team, and it was very difficult to get anyone to stand in for a colleague who happened to be away from work due to illness.

About 18 months previously the company had operated with three small independent order processing sections which had different salary scales, job titles, and apparent importance within the company. The decision was then taken to merge the three sections into one department to handle the processing of all orders received into the company, but the status differences were allowed to continue. Is it any wonder that the manager in charge is having difficulty building a team?

Many a day-to-day decision handled by managers at all levels also falls down for lack of thought. A serious case of this was seen after a manager had recruited a disabled person to work in the department which was located on the seventh floor of the office block. Ramps were provided for the wheelchair, and the lift was easily accessible—but what would happen if the building caught fire? How would the person in the wheelchair get out of the building? This could have been a disastrous oversight, made worse by the fact that the person would have been too heavy for many people to be able physically to assist down the stairs. Fortunately before any damage was done, arrangements were made to enable this person's work to be carried out on the ground floor.

The most recent example of this kind of thinking came to light when the safety officer of a company was addressing the staff on what to do if they discovered a bomb in the building. One of his recommended actions was to open all windows as soon as possible. Unfortunately the newly constructed building they were in complied with the architect's instructions to make the air conditioning system work efficiently; the win-

# FACTORS WHICH WILL INFLUENCE YOUR CHOICE OF ACTION

dows in the building were designed so that they could not be opened.

To minimize the likelihood of examples such as these, and many more, it is essential that the factors which are going to influence your choice of action are well thought through in detail. This is asking nothing more of you than what you would do quite automatically if you were going to spend your own money at home. For example, if you were going to buy a major item for your home you would want to be clear in your mind about the specific results you were looking for, the resources you were willing to commit, and any constraints which would have to be considered. In other words, all of the things that are important to you and to any other person who would be affected by the decision.

To illustrate this point let us look at a decision which many people have been involved with to some extent or another—the purchase of a house. The factors which would have influenced your choice could be listed, for example, as:

— Purchase price.
— Location/district.
— Size/shape of house.
— Number of rooms.
— Local amenities.
— Distance from place of work.
— Services available.
— Age of house.
— Size of garden.

Possibly there would be other factors, but the list would be a combination of all of the things that you and your partner considered important. Not only does this help to ensure that nothing is overlooked, it also makes your choice of action easier because the more accurately you paint the picture of what it is you are looking for, the easier it will be to recognize it when you see it.

For a working example let us apply these principles in full to the case study on the DM Organization, and the situation as we left it in chapter 2.

## DM Organization case study

We will assume that it was agreed that the lack of space was contributing to the majority of the problems the company was experiencing, and accept that the objective was to answer the question: 'What is the best way to overcome the space problem?'

With the objective clear, consideration must now be given to the factors which will influence the choice of action. It is all too easy to miss out this step and be guided by the enthusiasts who jump in with 'I know what we should do.' Very seldom are these people correct, and if it is you who will have to live with the decision you will be more confident if you take some time to think about the things which are vitally important—before you act.

Looking at the case study, it would appear that the factors which should be taken into consideration when overcoming the space problem could be listed like this:

– Costs.
– People involved.
– Profitability.
– Stock turnover.
– Product range.

# FACTORS WHICH WILL INFLUENCE YOUR CHOICE OF ACTION

- Current production.
- Company image.
- Return on capital employed.
- Sales.
- Market share.
- Safety.
- Local council approval.
- Company growth.

You may have thought of others which you would wish to consider, but the above list should be sufficient to demonstrate the process.

What needs to be done now is to extend each of the factors into statements which clearly and accurately specify the results required, the resources available, and any existing constraints. One way to do this is to complete the following sentence against each of the factors listed: 'Whichever method is chosen should.............................'

Applying this rule will enable you to provide a clear specification of what is required.

The following is an example of how this could be done with regard to the previous list of factors on the space problem.

| *Factor* | *Whichever method is chosen should:* |
|---|---|
| Costs | – Cost no more than £2.3 million. |
|  | – Be minimum cost possible. |
| People | – Be acceptable to the work force. |
|  | – Help to reduce management turnover. |
| Profitability | – Improve the profitability of the company. |

| Factor | Whichever method is chosen should: |
|---|---|
| Stock turnover | – Allow improved stock turnover. |
| Product range | – Allow retention of existing range. |
| | – Permit an increase of the range. |
| Current production | – Cause minimum disruption to production. |
| Company image | – Project best image. |
| Return on capital | – Provide best possible ROC. |
| Sales | – Cater for increased sales. |
| Market share | – Increase market share. |
| Safety | – Not require the company to reduce existing safety standards. |
| | – Allow improvement in safety record. |
| Local council | – Meet with local council agreement. |
| Company growth | – Cater for future growth of the company. |

This specification could now be used to see which option best meets the requirements of the company. If many ideas are put forward for consideration, however, it could be very time consuming to go through every one of the options to see how well each one satisfies the various needs. To reduce the time required for the comparison to be made, it is worth going back over the specification to identify any of the statements where it is mandatory that satisfaction is obtained for the decision to be acceptable. These essential factors can then be used as a sifting process to shortlist the options which are worth further consideration. For example, it would not be good use of your time to study in detail the benefits of an option which would cost £5.0 million if you only have £2.3 million to spend.

## FACTORS WHICH WILL INFLUENCE YOUR CHOICE OF ACTION

To establish which of the factors should be described as essential, you can apply the same sentence as earlier but this time use the word 'must' in place of 'should', where appropriate. The capital expenditure factor may then be expressed like this: 'Whichever method is chosen must not cost more than £2.3 million.' Before this is done, however, there are two cautions which have to be observed:

- When you classify a factor as 'essential' you must really mean it, otherwise it cannot be used for shortlisting options. You must be confident enough to say that if an option does not provide the satisfaction you have specified, it will not be looked at further.

- The more often you classify a factor as 'essential', the fewer options you will find to exist—be realistic.

The remaining factors are those which will be used to reflect the benefits and risks associated with each option when it is examined. Against each of these factors we will want to know how well we are satisfied with what the options provide.

An option which provides a great deal of benefit with very low risk will tend to look attractive, and we could easily be influenced by this to the point of making that option our choice. However, it is unlikely that each factor will carry the same importance and unless we are clear in our mind with regard to the relative importance of each of the factors, our judgement could be seriously distorted. Ideally we would like to see the benefits in the areas of high importance, and the risks in the less important areas.

By looking carefully through the list of factors which remain, it should be possible to identify the factor or factors which can be considered to be of maximum value with regard to the overall success of the decision. Now the factor(s) should be marked in such a way that it/they will be easily recognized as having top priority. Alternatively, as I prefer to do, start a new list with the most important factor at the top. Each of the remaining factors should now be assessed for its relative importance when compared to the one declared to be the top priority. All the factors can now be identified in such a way as to indicate their order of importance, by number or letter, or by writing them down in descending order of importance.

Returning to the DM Organization case study, where all the guidelines stated have been followed, we can examine a sample of a specification which could be used to resolve the space problem.

SAMPLE SPECIFICATION

Whichever method is chosen to overcome the space problem, it must:

– Cost no more than £2.3 million capital.
– Cater for the future growth needs of 15 per cent over five years.
– Meet with local council approval.
– Allow for the maintenance of existing safety standards.

Whichever method is chosen should also take into considera-

## FACTORS WHICH WILL INFLUENCE YOUR CHOICE OF ACTION

tion the benefits and risks associated with the following (listed in descending order of importance):

- Disruption to current production.
- The retention of the existing product range.
- Acceptance by the workforce.
- Assistance in improving stock turnover.
- Management turnover.
- Company profitability.
- New product range.
- Improved safety record.
- Sales volume.
- Return on capital employed.
- Market share.
- Company image.
- Amount of capital required.

Before a specification is used by anyone, it should be tested against the following questions.

- How realistic is the specification?
- Does the specification accurately provide a picture of what is required by all concerned?
- Is it balanced, or does it reflect an unfair emphasis towards finance, sales, production or personnel, for example?
- Is it fair, or does it tend to be a specification which would favour a particular option?

Positive replies to the questions will allow you to move into the search for options with real confidence.

## Guidelines for the development of factors which will influence your choice of action

- List the factors which are important to you, and to those who will be affected by the decision. These will normally be found under the following headings: people, organization, processes, materials, money, external influences, output or facilities.
- Extend the factors into statements which specify the results expected, resources available, or constraints which may exist. This can be done by completing the following sentence: 'Whichever method is chosen should ............................,'
- Classify the statements which will have to be regarded as essential. These essential factors will be the statements which are appropriate to the changed sentence: 'Whichever method is chosen must ............................'
- Assess the varying importance of the remaining factors and list them in descending order of importance (or by identifying each of them with a number or letter which will be easily recognized by yourself, and by anyone else who may be involved with making the choice).
- Check the completed specification against the following questions:
    - How realistic is it?
    - Does it paint a true picture of what is required?
    - How balanced is it?
    - How fair is it?

# 4.

# Generating options

Dependent upon the type of decision to be made, the search for methods to achieve the desired results will vary in difficulty, although the task will be made easier when there is a clear picture of what is required.

When the decision being worked on is the choice of a piece of equipment or service, the option will normally be found quite easily by reference to a directory of suppliers.

Should the decision be to do with the selection of a person to fill a particular vacancy, this may be tackled by reference to the company's manpower information, by an advertisement in the press, or by contacting an agency.

Choice of a new location for a branch office might be done by asking appropriate estate agents to furnish you with details of sites available.

The above examples are normally quite easy to handle because there are people whose main function is the compilation of records of such options. With the majority of decisions managers have to handle, however, a list of suitable options very seldom exists. Managers have to create this list as and when the situations arise. The more creative in our thinking we can become, the better our chances will be to generate an unbiased complete group of good ideas to choose from.

Much has been written on the subject of creative thinking and quite rightly so, because it is not just a neglected skill, it is a skill which life conditions us to reject. Young children are normally very inquisitive, imaginative, and creative but as they grow up they are conditioned to think within certain boundaries. 'We don't do that,' 'That won't work,' 'I'll show you what to do,' tend to be the norm in our education of young people. It is, of course, correct that we teach people certain rules, but if we are not careful we can discourage new thinking. It happens at work when a subordinate suggests a different way to do something. The boss has been heard to say that the employee is not paid to think. It's not always in those words—sometimes it is expressed as: 'It's against company policy,' or 'We wouldn't be allowed to do it that way,' or 'It's been tried before,' or 'We couldn't afford it.'

We do know that some of the greatest discoveries in the world were made by someone who was prepared to question the rules. At one stage in our history it was commonly accepted that the world was flat, and that only birds could fly. People who thought differently were not encouraged; they were actively discouraged from finding out if the rules were correct.

In general, therefore, it can be said that creativity is not stimulated. We are taught to think logically and to follow pre-set rules, which is excellent for most of the time but *new ideas* very seldom emerge from logical thinking.

Returning for a moment to young children, they ask a number of awkward questions because they lack knowledge

## GENERATING OPTIONS

but they have not yet been constrained in their quest for knowledge. A child's questions and its thinking are largely controlled by the emotional part of the brain. In other words, the child's behaviour is determined by any strong feeling it experiences. If a child does not know the reason for something it will innocently ask the question, regardless of who is present at the time, and it will add the tantalizing 'WHY?' if it is not satisfied with the answer. We do not lose this inquisitive desire for information because we obtain all the answers; we are more likely to do so as a result of conditioning of our minds which stifles our questioning.

Take the child who is accompanying its mother around a crowded supermarket. The child sees a rather strange looking and somewhat obese lady standing in front of them at the checkout desk. The child may wish to know why the lady is of the proportions she is and ask the question in a loud, clear voice: 'Mummy, why is that lady so ugly and fat?' Whatever the mother's reply, it is likely to include advice that it is rude to say things like that. This has the effect of developing what is often referred to as the logical or reasoning part of the brain, or the rules which control our emotional feelings. With the child, our hopes are that the next time the child has such a question the logical part of the brain will tell the emotional part that the mouth is not going to operate.

The child will then be said to be growing up, because its behaviour is being determined by logic and reason, and its emotion is under control.

At work, the same thing happens. A new employee may start off by asking why certain procedures are followed, and suggesting different ways to do things. Should that person perceive that in this company the definition of a good employee is used for people who do as they are told without questioning the rules, creativity will be shut off.

As *creative* is defined as having 'originality of thought and showing imagination', *emotion* being derived from the Latin *'emovere'*, meaning 'to disturb', it seems correct to suggest that if we wish to be more creative we should occasionally disturb the boundaries which have been laid down in our minds.

There is a technique called brainstorming which can be very useful for disturbing these boundaries and letting our creativity develop. The results can be quite astounding, with ideas which might never have been thought of coming to the surface for consideration.

It is possible to brainstorm for options on your own, although for best results it is recommended that it is carried out by a small group of, say, four to ten people. The members of the group can be from very diverse functions within the company but they must have trust and confidence in each other for it to work well.

Quite simply, you state your objective to the group and invite anyone to voice any idea which comes to mind to meet the objective, however costly, stupid, impossible, illegal, immoral, or unprofitable the idea may seem to be. No one is permitted to reason an idea at this stage by saying that it won't work, it's been tried before, or it wouldn't be permitted. What must be allowed to happen—in fact positively encouraged—is that a free-rolling emotional brain should throw in as many ideas as possible.

All ideas should be written out if possible on a paper board or blackboard, as the visual record can spark off other ideas,

## GENERATING OPTIONS

with the back-up of a tape recorder in case the ideas are coming so fast that they cannot all be written down as they are said. Use the tape recording *after* the session to check that all ideas are written out, because it can stop the flow of ideas to do so during the session.

Only when the ideas appear to be really exhausted, which could be between 10 and 20 minutes, should you start to apply a more logical approach to the situation.

Look back over the list of ideas and examine each one in detail to establish that it is complying with legality, morality and company ethics, as well as the factors which you previously determined to be essential, like capital expenditure and profitability limits. This will provide you with various courses of action which could be looked at further:

- As the idea stands it should be included as an option to be fully evaluated.

- The idea with slight modifications could be included as an option to be fully evaluated.

- This idea, combined with one or two more, could make a viable option.

- The idea as it stands should be ruled out completely, although it seems to have a germ of an idea, which if looked at from another angle may produce a worthwhile option.

or
- The idea is totally impractical and will be ruled out.

Practice with this approach to generating options, whether as an individual or with other people to help you, does stimulate creativity. Like any other skill, however, it has to be applied positively to produce the results.

To be fair, of course, it must be recognized that fear plays its part in discouraging creativity. The fear of suggesting new ideas is often expressed: 'Oh, that's a big step to take,' or 'I couldn't risk trying that out because we've not been involved with such a change.' These are only valid concerns if you are being asked to implement an idea without comparing it with the factors which were deemed to be important to the success of the decision.

Creativity is necessary for the generation of options, *not* for making the decision. When you are looking for ideas for the achievement of an objective, there should be no reason for you to be afraid to include options which you just 'feel' would not be acceptable. For example, you may believe that no action should be taken and the situation would be best if it remained unaltered.

In chapter 5 we will deal with the comparison of options with the factors which will influence the final choice. Options, including the status quo, should at least have the opportunity to prove or disprove their worth.

With the case study on the DM Organization, a mini brainstorm could provide us with the following list of options.

A   Expand the manufacturing area into a second floor by building upwards.

B   Extend the manufacturing area on to the sports field.

C   Reduce the product range.

## GENERATING OPTIONS

D   Move the offices to a new location and use the space freed by this to increase manufacturing space.

E   Move entirely to new premises.

F   Put in a major change to the company's layout in the existing area.

G   Improve the raw material stock control system, to free some warehouse space for manufacturing.

H   Status quo.

This is not intended to be an exhaustive list, just a sample for us to work on as a case study. Should you think of other options which you would like to look at, please add them to the list. You will be able to see how they compare in the following chapter.

# 5.

# Comparing the options and making the choice

Very seldom, if at all, when making decisions will the perfect answer be found. Compromise or balance has to be sought between the satisfaction of factors which are often at variance with each other. For example, the satisfaction of economic factors by an option may at the same time cause dissatisfaction with regard to some human factors. Or options which offer extremely attractive benefits may also involve a very high risk element. They all have to be examined carefully in order for it to be possible to arrive at the best-balanced choice.

The difficulty is usually experienced when options offer, for example:

— Improvements in morale, at the price of requiring a large cash injection.
— Allowing a cutback on expenses, at the price of upsetting *some* of the staff.
— Improvements in customer satisfaction, at the price of adding difficulty to manufacturing.

- A reduction in budgeted expenses, at the price of causing damage to safety records.
- Improvement in maintenance, at the price of slowing production down.
- Improvement in quality, at the price of adding to manufacturing costs
- Improvement in efficiency, at the price of requiring more/less people to be employed.
- Savings on insurance costs, at the price of imposing restrictions on smoking.

Arriving at the compromise which is the best available from all aspects and viewpoints need not be as difficult as it seems to be at first. Compromise can only be made with regard to degrees of satisfaction with benefits and risks. No compromise should take place in areas where it was previously agreed that the factors were mandatory for the decision to be successful.

The first stage in the comparison of options, therefore, is to eliminate those options which would require compromise to be made in areas which were specified as essential. Quite simply this means that if an option fails to satisfy any essential factor it must be dispensed with straight away, leaving the time available to be most efficiently and effectively utilized comparing only the options where compromise is possible. Those are the options which match the limits of results, resources, and constraints.

Using the DM Organization case study, we can see how the process works. For the purpose of demonstration we can use the factors which were developed in chapter 3, and see how the options generated in chapter 4 satisfy the requirements. I will also be using information which you would

# COMPARING THE OPTIONS AND MAKING THE CHOICE

normally have access to, therefore any conclusions drawn will only represent an example of how the process can be applied.

## DM Organization case study

As the first stage in the comparison of options is to ensure that options satisfy the essential factors, let us remind ourselves what these were.

It was agreed that whichever method is chosen to overcome the space problem must
– Cost no more than £2.3 million.
– Cater for future growth needs of 15 per cent over five years.
– Meet with local council approval.
– Allow for maintenance of existing safety standards.

Examining each option in turn, we get the following results.

*Expanding upwards*
– Would cost £360 000.
– Provision of additional 70 per cent manufacturing space.
– Local council will not permit because of residential area.
– No reasons for safety standards to fall.

*Use of sports field*
– Would cost £162 000.
– Provision of additional 25 per cent usable space.
– Building permission no problem.
– No reasons for safety standards to fall.

*Reduce product range*
– No capital costs.
– Releases overall 20 per cent manufacturing space.

- Council not involved.
- No reason for safety standards to fall.

*Move offices*
- Local authority offices available for lease but capital to convert offices into factory would be £35 000.
- Provision of additional 10 per cent manufacturing space.
- Council welcomes the idea.
- Increased travel between units would increase safety hazards but can be catered for.

*Move entire factory*
- Estimated costs of £2 million.
- No problem for growth if new site is available.
- Council encouraging businesses to take up offers of land for sale.
- Safety standards could be improved.

*Change the company layout*
- Estimated costs of £89 000.
- Could recover 15 per cent space.
- Council not involved.
- Safety standards could be maintained.

*Improve stock control*
- Estimated cost of £22 000.
- Would recover five per cent space.
- Council not involved.
- No reason why safety standards should fall.

*Status quo*
- No costs involved.
- Would not be able to grow.
- Council not involved.
- Safety standards could be maintained.

## COMPARING THE OPTIONS AND MAKING THE CHOICE

For convenience, we can give the results of this stage of the comparison using a simple matrix, as shown in Fig. 5.1.

| Essential factors | EXPAND UPWARDS | USE SPORTS FIELD | REDUCE PRODUCT RANGE | MOVE OFFICES | MOVE ENTIRE FACTORY | CHANGE COMPANY LAYOUT | IMPROVE STOCK CONTROL | STATUS QUO |
|---|---|---|---|---|---|---|---|---|
| MAXIMUM CAPITAL OF £2.3M | ✓ | ✓ | ✓ | ✓ | ✓ | ✓ | ✓ | ✓ |
| FUTURE GROWTH OF 15% | ✓ | ✓ | ✓ | ✗ | ✓ | ✓ | ✗ | ✗ |
| MEET COUNCIL APPROVAL | ✗ | ✓ | ✓ | ✓ | ✓ | ✓ | ✓ | ✓ |
| MAINTAIN SAFETY STANDARDS | ✓ | ✓ | ✓ | ✓ | ✓ | ✓ | ✓ | ✓ |

**Figure 5.1** Comparison of the options and the essential factors

It can be seen from Fig. 5.1 that we are left with only four options to look at further. What needs to be done now, therefore, is to collect the information about the four remaining options to see how they compare.

As the information is collected, an assessment of the degree of satisfaction of benefits and risks associated with each option needs to be carried out in a way that will allow an objective and fair comparison to be made.

There are a number of ways to do this and of course you should develop a system which suits you, but it must be a consistent method which fairly reflects the benefit and risk. Using symbols which describe your understanding of the extent to which each option caters for your requirements will allow the matrix to be extended to show the complete picture, which is more convenient than having to keep referring back to each option when comparison is being made.

For example:

H   could be used to denote your high satisfaction where the option provides maximum benefit, or the total absence of risk.

M   could be used to signify medium satisfaction, where benefits and risks are reasonable.

L   could be used to describe low satisfaction, where minimal benefit is provided, or high risk is involved.

N   could denote no satisfaction where no benefit or very high risk exists.

X   could signify the fact that the option is actually working against you in this regard by taking benefit away or by introducing unreasonably high risk.

To put this into practice with the DM case study, I will record information which could be applicable to the various options, and against each piece of data an assessment of the degree of satisfaction (see Fig. 5.2). A reminder of the factors we are using, listed in descending order of priority, is given below and on pages 62–64.

– Disruption to current production.
– Retention of existing product range.
– Acceptability by the workforce.

# COMPARING THE OPTIONS AND MAKING THE CHOICE

Options to be considered:
- EXPAND UPWARDS
- USE SPORTS FIELD
- REDUCE PRODUCT RANGE
- MOVE OFFICES
- MOVE ENTIRE FACTORY
- CHANGE COMPANY LAYOUT
- IMPROVE STOCK CONTROL
- STATUS QUO

**Essential factors**

| | Expand Upwards | Use Sports Field | Reduce Product Range | Move Offices | Move Entire Factory | Change Company Layout | Improve Stock Control | Status Quo |
|---|---|---|---|---|---|---|---|---|
| MAXIMUM CAPITAL OF £2.3M | ✓ | ✓ | ✓ | ✓ | ✓ | ✓ | ✓ | ✓ |
| FUTURE GROWTH OF 15% | ✓ | ✓ | ✓ | ✗ | ✓ | ✓ | ✗ | ✗ |
| MEET COUNCIL APPROVAL | ✗ | ✓ | ✓ | ✓ | ✓ | ✓ | ✓ | ✓ |
| MAINTAIN SAFETY STANDARDS | ✓ | ✓ | ✓ | ✓ | ✓ | ✓ | ✓ | ✓ |

**Benefit/risk**

| | | | | | | | | |
|---|---|---|---|---|---|---|---|---|
| DISRUPTION TO PRODUCTION | | H | H | | M | L | | |
| RETENTION OF RANGE | | H | ✗ | | H | H | | |
| ACCEPTABLE BY WORKFORCE | | ✗ | M | | ✗ | M | | |
| IMPROVED STOCK TURNOVER | | H | H | | H | M | | |
| MANAGEMENT TURNOVER | | M | N | | H | N | | |
| COMPANY PROFITABILITY | | M | L | | M | L | | |
| NEW PRODUCTS | | M | L | | H | L | | |
| IMPROVED SAFETY | | H | M | | H | M | | |
| SALES VOLUME | | H | L | | M | L | | |
| RETURN ON CAPITAL | | M | H | | M | M | | |
| MARKET SHARE | | M | ✗ | | M | L | | |
| COMPANY IMAGE | | L | ✗ | | H | L | | |
| AMOUNT OF CAPITAL USED | | H | H | | L | H | | |

**Figure 5.2** The completed matrix which can be used for the comparison of the options

61

- Assistance to improving stock turnover situation.
- Management turnover.
- Company profitability.
- New products for the future.
- Improvement to safety record.
- Sales volume.
- Return on capital employed.
- Market share.
- Company image
- Amount of capital required.

*The option to use the sports field*
- Would not disrupt the current production.                H
- Could retain existing range.                             H
- The workforce would be very upset.                       X
- Stock control system could be improved.                  H
- Increased chance for management prospects.               M
- Could increase company profitability.                    M
- Room for some addition to the product range.             M
- Safety record could improve.                             H
- Sales volume could increase.                             H
- Return on capital, five years.                           M
- Market share could increase by five per cent.            M
- Local press coverage of removal of sports field
  could damage that part of company image.                 L
- Seven per cent of available capital required.            H

*The option to reduce the product range*
- Would not disrupt production.                            H
- Could not keep existing range.                           X
- Workforce may not be involved.                           M
- Stock control would be much easier.                      H
- No benefit towards management turnover.                  N
- Could marginally improve profitability.                  L

## COMPARING THE OPTIONS AND MAKING THE CHOICE

| | |
|---|---|
| – May allow future new products. | L |
| – Would help safety records. | M |
| – Sales volume may not change. | L |
| – No capital involved. | H |
| – Overall market share may drop. | X |
| – Some customers would not like it. | X |

*The option to move factory and offices*

| | |
|---|---|
| – If new place built and equipped before the move, there would be minimal disruption. | M |
| – Existing range easily maintained. | H |
| – Workforce could be opposed to moving. | X |
| – New system of stock control could be put in. | H |
| – With scope for real growth, management prospects could be improved. | H |
| – Overall profitability could be improved. | M |
| – Scope for new products. | H |
| – Improved safety no difficulty. | H |
| – Sales volume could be increased. | M |
| – Return on capital: two years by sale of existing factory, and five years on the balance. | M |
| – Market share could increase. | M |
| – Good image if move is handled well, and new premises blend in with environment. | H |
| – All available capital would be required. | L |

*The option to change the layout of the company*

| | |
|---|---|
| – Would cause disruption to production. | L |
| – Existing range could be maintained. | H |
| – Workforce may not object, but could be pleased. | M |
| – Stock control could be improved. | M |
| – No real impact on management prospects. | N |
| – Could marginally improve profitability. | L |

## IMPROVE YOUR DECISION MAKING SKILLS

- Not much help for new products.   L
- Could allow safety to improve.   M
- Slight help for sales volume.   L
- Return on capital in three years.   M
- Marginal impact on market share.   L
- May improve company image.   L
- Amount of capital required is 3.8 per cent of that available.   H

It would be a mistake, of course, simply to look at the various options and count up to see which one provides the greatest number of high benefits, or the lowest number of risks. While this can give an indication with regard to the option which appears to be better than the others, it must be remembered that the benefit and risk factors will not very often be of equal importance. Additionally, there could be potential risks in the degree of satisfaction an option provides regarding the essential factors, if satisfaction is very close to the limit set.

To ensure that the likelihood of achieving the declared objective is the best possible, and that the resources are going to be utilized most productively, it is worth applying a little constructive pessimism—before commitment is made.

Answering objectively the following questions will help you to make a choice in which you can be confident.

- To what extent are you sure with regard to the validity of the information provided and its source?
- What are the implications of being close to limits with regard to the satisfaction of an essential factor?
- How confident are you that the assessment of satisfaction regarding benefit and risk is fair?

## COMPARING THE OPTIONS AND MAKING THE CHOICE

- To what extent can benefit be achieved in areas which were stated to be of high importance?
- To what extent is low benefit or high risk shown to be in areas of high importance?
- If you were to choose one of the options, could it have implications with regard to anything else you have under way?
- Are any risks identified likely to be serious enough to cause an option to be eliminated, or is it possible to develop a plan which could remove the risk, or at least minimize its effects, should the benefits warrant this action?

Applying these questions to each of the four options in the DM case study will assist in demonstrating their usefulness. (In this instance please accept that the validity of the information and its source are verified, and that the assessments made are regarded as fair!)

The question which deals with being close to limits only applies to two options: moving premises and changing the company layout. The other two options are considered all right in this regard.

Moving to a new location is estimated to cost £2 million, which is 87 per cent of the stated limit.

Changing the company layout is said to allow the 15 per cent growth required. If this is found to be over-optimistic, there could be difficulties.

To highlight these potential risk areas, and any others revealed by the remaining questions, the matrix can be marked in a way which draws attention to areas which could cause difficulties, as in Fig. 5.3.

# IMPROVE YOUR DECISION MAKING SKILLS

**Essential factors**

| | EXPAND UPWARDS | USE SPORTS FIELD | REDUCE PRODUCT RANGE | MOVE OFFICES | MOVE ENTIRE FACTORY | CHANGE COMPANY LAYOUT | IMPROVE STOCK CONTROL | STATUS QUO |
|---|---|---|---|---|---|---|---|---|
| MAXIMUM CAPITAL OF £2.3M | ✓ | ✓ | ✓ | ✓ | ⊘ | ✓ | ✓ | ✓ |
| FUTURE GROWTH OF 15% | ✓ | ✓ | ✓ | ✗ | ✓ | ⊘ | ✗ | ✗ |
| MEET COUNCIL APPROVAL | ✗ | ✓ | ✓ | ✓ | ✓ | ✓ | ✓ | ✓ |
| MAINTAIN SAFETY STANDARDS | ✓ | ✓ | ✓ | ✓ | ✓ | ✓ | ✓ | ✓ |

**Benefit/risk**

| | | | | | | | | |
|---|---|---|---|---|---|---|---|---|
| DISRUPTION TO PRODUCTION | | H | H | | M | Ⓛ | | |
| RETENTION OF RANGE | | H | ⓧ | | H | H | | |
| ACCEPTABLE BY WORKFORCE | | ⓧ | M | | ⓧ | M | | |
| IMPROVED STOCK TURNOVER | | H | H | | H | M | | |
| MANAGEMENT TURNOVER | | M | Ⓝ | | H | Ⓝ | | |
| COMPANY PROFITABILITY | | M | Ⓛ | | M | Ⓛ | | |
| NEW PRODUCTS | | M | Ⓛ | | H | Ⓛ | | |
| IMPROVED SAFETY | | H | M | | H | M | | |
| SALES VOLUME | | H | Ⓛ | | M | Ⓛ | | |
| RETURN ON CAPITAL | | M | H | | M | M | | |
| MARKET SHARE | | M | ⓧ | | M | Ⓛ | | |
| COMPANY IMAGE | | Ⓛ | ⓧ | | H | Ⓛ | | |
| AMOUNT OF CAPITAL USED | | H | H | | Ⓛ | H | | |

**Figure 5.3** Potential risk areas

## COMPARING THE OPTIONS AND MAKING THE CHOICE

Each of the areas highlighted can now be examined in depth to see if there is an option which could be recommended.

The option to use the sports field to extend the factory shows a great deal of benefit, with risk in the non-acceptance by the workforce, and the resultant adverse publicity in the press should it get that far. It may be able to overcome these if there is a sports field nearby which would be suitable to purchase for the employees' use. The remaining benefits suggest this could be worthy of examination.

Reducing the product range offers very little benefit, in fact, and as there is increasing demand for the entire range it would be a negative step to take.—Suggest option be eliminated.

Moving the entire factory to a new location has two potentially unsatisfactory elements. One is the amount of capital required, and the other is the workforce's likely reluctance to accept the idea.

With regard to the capital required, the amount estimated to be needed is 13 per cent less than the limit stated, and the amount of money required was said to be the least important factor as long as it was below the limit of £2.3 million. The option should not therefore be rejected on financial grounds. The potentially more serious factor is non-acceptance by the workforce, because the company is more than satisfied with the quality of the people it employs. Should moving result in the company losing a high percentage of the existing work force, it would not be a good option at all. However, if the move could be restricted to a distance which would mean that the existing workforce could be retained without extra cost or inconvenience, then the option should be considered.

The option to lay out the factory differently offers very little benefit with quite a great deal of risk. Future growth may be overly restricted and the disruption to existing production would be very difficult to cope with. The absence of benefit from some of the remaining factors would suggest that the company could be in the same situation again before very long.—Suggest option be eliminated.

This leaves two good options to choose from: use the sports field, or move to a new location completely. The long-term benefits could sway the decision in favour of the move, provided that the decision to choose the best location for the new factory considers 'near to existing factory' as a very important factor so that the existing workforce *can* be retained.

While we have been concentrating on the DM case study to demonstrate the process of comparing options, the principles apply in the same way to any other decision you might have to make.

I recall a colleague of mine some years ago mentioning that he was going to promote one of his team into a vacant position one step higher in the organization structure. I must have betrayed my feelings when he told me of his choice—I did not *feel* that it was a good decision. I questioned his objective and was asking what he had taken into consideration to arrive at his conclusion when he said to me: 'You're putting me through decision making, are you not?' I had to admit that I was, but my colleague said that he was quite happy to be questioned.

We reached the stage of being clear on the objective, clear

## COMPARING THE OPTIONS AND MAKING THE CHOICE

in our minds with regard to the factors important, and classified some of the factors as essential and assessed the importance of the remaining benefit/risk factors, all within approximately 20 minutes.

The following 20 minutes were used to compare the five natural candidates. In the end the best-balanced choice from the five candidates turned out to be the person he had chosen without formally going through the decision making process.

I apologized for taking up so much of his time on a decision that he had quite obviously handled on his own most effectively. His reply restored my faith because he said 'But I'm much more confident in my choice now than I would have been if you had not forced me to think it through properly.'

The worst that can happen as a result of taking the time to think the decision through is confirmation that your original decision was correct. The benefits to be gained if the best-balanced choice is *not* what you thought it to be don't need to be spelled out, do they?

### Guidelines for the comparison and choice

— Eliminate options which fail to meet essential limits.

— Collect information with regard to the benefit and risk factors for the remaining options.

— Assess the degree of satisfaction each option provides, e.g.:

    H   High satisfaction from maximum benefit or zero risk.
    M   Medium satisfaction from reasonable benefit or risk.
    L   Low satisfaction from minimal benefit or high risk.

## IMPROVE YOUR DECISION MAKING SKILLS

    N    No satisfaction from no benefit or very high risk.
    X    Removes existing benefit or introduces unreasonably high risk.

- Recheck the validity of the information provided.
- Ensure that satisfaction towards an essential factor is not too close to the limit set.
- Recheck for fair assessment of satisfaction against benefit/risk factors.
- Ensure that benefits provided are in the areas of high importance.
- Ensure that high risks and low benefits are not in the areas of high importance.
- Check to see if there could be implications with regard to other things under way, if a certain option is chosen.
- Question if risks identified are serious enough for an option to be eliminated, or is it possible to develop a plan which could remove the risk or minimize its effect.
- Select the best-balanced choice.
- If the best option available does not provide sufficient satisfaction with regard to benefits and risks, do not be afraid to look again for more options. Choosing the best from a selection of poor options will seldom be the wisest thing to do.

# 6.

## Presenting the recommendation

I can recall a very frustrated manager who wanted his company to spend £100 000 to improve security arrangements. The manager had done his homework and his case was very sound indeed.

For several years this manager had been raising requests to be allowed to include the expenditure in his budget, each time to no avail. In his frustrated state he explained to me why the company needed to improve its security with regard to the control of goods coming in and going out of the company, how the costs involved could be justified, and how quickly the company would see the return on its investment. He was right on all counts.

The situation briefly stated was this:

The company started business in 1936, and is now classed as medium sized, although it is part of a very large multinational organization. One of the security controls is a weighbridge which has to record the weight of all goods vehicles coming in and going out. On exit the only difference allowed is plus or minus the weight of the goods collected or delivered.

The manager went on to explain that when the weighbridge had been installed many years previously, its physical size was all right for the size of vehicles in those days, but now vehicles are up to four times larger, and could not fit on to the weighbridge. The result of this was that a vehicle had to be weighed two or three times. First the front axles would be weighed, then the next set of axles would be weighed, and on some occasions with the very large vehicles a third weighing was necessary. After a complex calculation was made with the two or three readings, a weight was written on to a piece of paper which was handed to the driver. The driver was then asked if this was the correct weight of the vehicle, and, depending on his relationship with the gate keeper, he would agree, or suggest a different figure.

The £100 000 was the cost of installing a new weighbridge which would be compatible with the size of vehicles using it, thereby accurately controlling this part of security for the company. As the company was manufacturing attractive products which had an easy secondhand market, a conservative estimate of savings by the improved security was said to be £50 000 per year.

The multi-national organization operated a project system, whereby all requests for expenditure over a certain figure required the completion of a project request form, which then had to be sent to head office for approval.

Examination of the files in the project control department, revealed that there were many requests on file for the new weighbridge and each one was marked 'rejected'. Looking at each of the requests in turn was quite astonishing and certainly provided no surprise at their rejection, although I often wondered why no one had questioned them. In the part

## PRESENTING THE RECOMMENDATION

of the request form where information had to be supplied with regard to why the money was needed, this manager had on each occasion completed the section with the words 'The existing system is out of date.'

There was nothing wrong with the manager's ability to analyse a situation, or to work out what was needed, but he was totally lacking in the way he presented his recommendation. How often do we also fail in this essential part of our job?

Our failure can be brought about by not providing the information required, as in the previous example, or it can be due to the provision of the information in a biased way. Whichever it is can be very costly in time wasted. Managers often tell me that they do not have enough time available to do their job properly—so why waste it?

Take this example of a company which was in very keen direct competition with another. Both companies were supplying a major consumer with their products and their share of this consumer's business varied month to month around 53 per cent and 47 per cent.

The sales director of one of the companies explained that he wanted to be allowed to increase his sales budget to improve sales over the competitor.

The engineering design director's argument was to agree a 50:50 share of the consumer's business with the competitor, thereby reducing the need to spend money on sales in this area, and allowing both companies to share technological information.

The argument went on and on at every meeting the two directors attended, but no decision was ever agreed. Eventually the managing director instructed the two directors to get together to examine the situation objectively to determine the best way to handle this consumer's business (objective clear). He added: '... and I want your presentation at our next meeting to include *all* the factors you considered, plus the options open to us, and your combined recommendations which show the benefits and the risks to the company.'

The decision was finalized at the next meeting, implemented within six weeks, and no more time was *wasted* on the subject.

To increase your success in getting approval to proceed with your recommendations, practise the skills of presenting information in a formal situation. When the information has to be presented informally the adjustment is easier in this direction

For many people, the biggest personal communication challenge of all is addressing a group of others, and yet for a manager it is vital to be able to do this competently. It is very often the most effective way to present recommendations because you can be addressing all the people who will be affected by the decision, or at least a representative sample. You will be able therefore to obtain immediate reaction and feedback which will allow you to develop any aspects which require it, where necessary change the emphasis, or further clarify points as they arise.

To be successful in presenting information to others requires good preparation. There is no substitute for this.

**The rules of preparation**

– Clarify your objective. What has to be achieved as a result of your presentation? Is it to obtain the commitment of the group that your solution as it stands should be implemented? Or is it to provide the opportunity to invite other options for comparison during the presentation? Or is it to make your recommendation for others to pass on to a higher level?

— Consider your audience. What type of people are they? What knowledge will they possess? Are they likely to be receptive or not? What do you know of their general attitudes? Try to look at the subject from the audience's point of view and plan to present in a way that is most suited to them, rather than the way you would like to do it.

— Decide on the content of your presentation. What must be included? What should be included? And, if time permits, what could be included? It is the third category which provides flexibility for time control during the presentation.

— Draw up a framework for the presentation. How will you introduce the subject? How will the central theme be developed? How will you close? An example of a framework development for a presentation of recommendations could be as follows:

State the objective worked on.
Explain the factors which were considered important to all concerned.
Outline the options generated.
Explain what is proposed.
Provide reasons for choice.
Seek commitment.
Arrive at agreement on follow-up action.

— Decide if any visual aids will be beneficial. A chart, a graph, or a matrix showing the comparison of options often takes less time and can cause more information to be assimilated than words alone.

— Prepare notes for reference during your presentation. These will help you to stay on track, and will reinforce your confidence. Make sure, however, that the notes only have your key points to remember, otherwise you may be tempted to try to read to the audience. It is difficult to sound convincing when notes are read, and you will lose the opportunity to see the reaction in the faces of your audience.

— Check the venue to be used. What facilities will you require? What will be the best seating arrangements? Give yourself time—don't leave it until the last minute.

— Depending on the importance of the recommendation, and the frequency with which you make presentations, practice is always useful, especially if you practise with a recorder, audio or video, so that you can review your presentation before anyone else.

The prerequisites to successful presentations are confidence and commitment. Your confidence will be enhanced if you have prepared well, but your commitment will be assessed by the manner of your presentation. If you don't sound convinced by your own case, it will be difficult for anyone else to go along with you. On the other hand, appearing to be too enthusiastic could cause people to become suspicious of your argument.

Following the guidelines for presenting the recommendation will help you to project the correct balance.

PRESENTING THE RECOMMENDATION

## Presentation guidelines

- Be yourself. Do not try to imitate a speaker you've known, as you will be seen to be acting and you will lose credibility. Ensure that you use words that you are familiar with, and let your true personality come through in a natural way.

- Open strongly. Try to get the attention of your audience straight away, don't just drift into your presentation. People may know why you are making the presentation, but restating the objective you have been working on will ensure that everyone is totally clear with regard to the relevance of what is to follow. If you wish to make your presentation and take questions at the end, tell your audience straight away. Also tell them if you are going to provide written back-up documentation at the end of your presentation. Your audience will then be able to listen to your presentation without wondering if they were supposed to interrupt with questions, or whether they should be making notes.

- Present clearly and naturally. Don't be tempted to rush, give yourself time to breathe, and use pauses to make sure you have enough breath for your next sentence.

    Speak to your audience, eye to eye, and spread your eye contact around. This way you are letting everyone know you are including them in your presentation, and you can see how your information is being accepted.

    Sometimes the clarity of voice is spoiled by a dryness in the throat. Should you think that a glass of water would be useful during your presentation, have one ready before you start—and don't be afraid to take the time to take a drink when you need it.

- Develop and proceed logically. The framework you developed during your preparation should be followed in its logical sequence, linking each point to the next one so that you have a smooth and obviously well-prepared presentation.
- Try not to distract your audience. If you come over naturally some mannerisms will never be noticed. However, excessive hand waving or money jingling, or the regular and frequent use of the same word or gesture can have your audience counting these instead of listening to you.
- Maintain audience concentration. Possibly the best way to cause people to concentrate on what you are saying is to ensure that they know what is in it for them. By showing how you have considered a balanced list of factors which includes items of importance to your audience, you will increase the likelihood of maintaining a desire to listen.
- Close positively. In this application final impressions are more important than first impressions. Leave your audience with the message, don't fade away. You need their commitment: ask for it. You need to know who is going to follow up with action: ask for it.

# 7.

# Planning for implementation

On the shelves of managers throughout the country, recommendations to remove some of the difficulties and improve some inefficient systems can be seen collecting dust. The people involved did not know they had a responsibility for action, or more likely they simply assumed that someone else was looking after it.

In an organization which possibly employs the greatest number of people in the UK, a young lady put forward a simple suggestion which would show savings in the administrative running costs of the organization. The new procedure did not require any money to be spent to make it work, it did not cause anyone to lose their job, and it did not detract from efficiency in any way.

The savings were calculated to be several thousands of pounds per year, and the young lady was awarded over £2000 for her contribution. . . . Four years later, the old procedure still trundles on!

In this example the young lady who put forward the suggestion was in a junior clerical function, and it would be unreasonable to expect her to follow up with action to make it work. But what was her supervisor doing? Or that person's supervisor?

If you are involved with or have taken the trouble to make a positive recommendation which will benefit the company and the people in the company, and your recommendation has been accepted, then also assume some responsibility to ensure that your decision becomes effective.

There are many good books on planning techniques. The objective of this short chapter is simply to remind you of those vital planning skills which are essential if the time you have taken to make a good decision is going to provide you with the best return.

## Implementation guidelines

- Plan the sequence of events. This requires someone to look at the events which have to be undertaken, and to lay down a logical sequence for them to be carried out if the decision is to be implemented on schedule.
- Set target dates. Each event should be allocated a time frame, specifying when it is possible to start and when it should be finished. This allows others involved to schedule their responsibilities in line with their resources.
- Assign responsibilities. Someone has to take overall responsibility to ensure that implementation stays on schedule. To do this, that person must know who has the responsibility for each event, and each person must know precisely what is expected.

    Overlapping responsibility on the assumption that it acts as a safeguard does not very often achieve this. It is

## PLANNING FOR IMPLEMENTATION

more likely that one person will think that the other is doing it, so it does not get done at all.

- Set up monitoring systems. Plans are projections of what should happen. Given that conditions are unlikely to be exactly as anticipated, it is necessary to have a system which provides feedback on progress. This should be the most practical but simple method of keeping you informed of the progress of each event.

- Re-examine the critical events. What has been covered so far in the guidelines is commonly known as planning for what should happen. Successful managers do not leave it at that, they also plan for what could happen. This requires a thorough examination of the crucial elements in the plan and an assessment made of any potential problems which could emerge. Action to avoid or at least contain the effect to a minimum also has to be catered for in the plan.

# 8.

# Making it happen for you

This book has covered some very simple straightforward principles which when applied to decisions you will face in business, or at home, will assure you of increased success. As you do improve your decision making skills and achieve an increased success rate you will find that you will be involved with fewer problems. Your colleagues, seeing you under less pressure than they are, may accuse you of being lucky.

A famous golfer was said to be lucky when he won the American Open Championship with a very long finishing putt which if he had missed would have resulted in a play-off. His reply to the person who had said he was lucky was: 'Yes, I suppose that is true, but I do find that my luck increases the more I practise.' You could use the same reply to your colleagues if you practise the skills for improving your decision making. The following pages are designed to help you to do just that.

Start by thinking of a decision you are currently working on and put the complete decision making process to work for you. Alternatively, take a decision you have made recently and find out whether you did arrive at the best-balanced choice available.

## Clarify your objective

Describe the situation you are working on, state your precise objective, and test it against the guidelines in chapter 2.

MAKING IT HAPPEN FOR YOU

## Consider the factors which will influence your choice of action

List the factors important to you and to those affected by the decision.




Extend the factors into statements which specify the results expected, resources available, or constraints which may exist. Complete the following sentence for each factor listed.

Whichever method is chosen should ................................

Classify the statements which will have to be regarded as essential.

Whichever method is chosen must ..................................




Assess the varying importance of the remaining factors and list them in descending order of importance.

# MAKING IT HAPPEN FOR YOU

Write out the completed specification.

Check the specification.
How realistic is it?
Does it paint a true picture of what is required?
How balanced is it?
How fair is it?

Generate the options which could be compared with your completed specification. Do not forget to include the status quo as an option.

Compare the options against your essential factors.

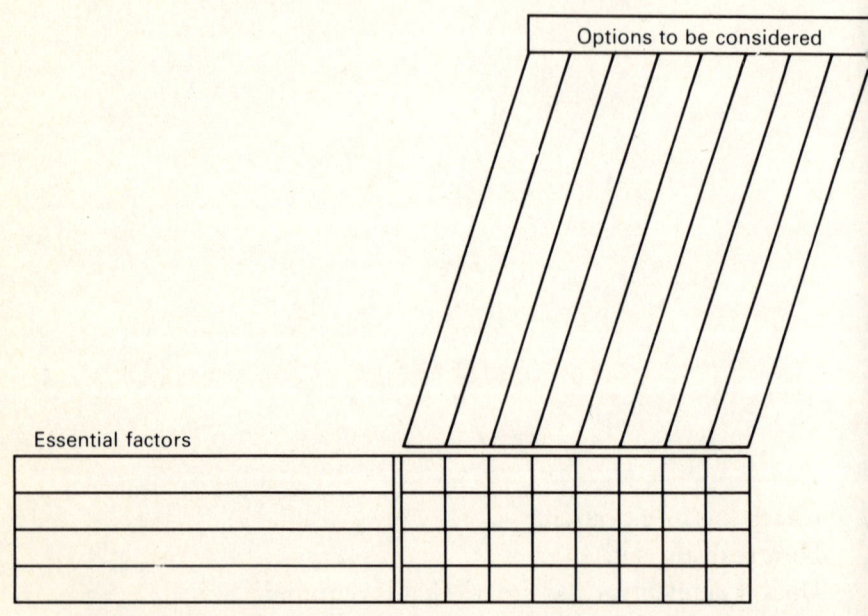

**Figure 8.1** Blank matrix for the comparison of options to essential factors

Collect information with regard to the benefit and risk factors for the remaining options, and assess the degree of satisfaction each option provides.

# IMPROVE YOUR DECISION MAKING SKILLS

Complete your matrix in order that a general comparison can be made.

Options to be considered

Essential factors

Benefit/risk

**Figure 8.2** Blank matrix for the complete comparison of remaining options

Identify risk areas.




Describe your best-balanced choice.

## Prepare for your presentation of recommended action

What will your objective be?




What do you know about the people you will be presenting to?




State the content of your presentation:

Must include ..................................

Should include ..................................

Could include ..................................

**MAKING IT HAPPEN FOR YOU**

Draw up the framework for your presentation:

Opening ........................................

Central theme development ........................................

Closing ........................................

What visual aids will be useful to you to explain more clearly, or quickly?

Prepare your notes with key points to aid your memory.

What venue will you use, and what facilities will you require?

MAKING IT HAPPEN FOR YOU

## Plan for the implementation

Sequence of events




Target dates




Assigned responsibilities




Monitoring systems

What potential problems could exist in the crucial areas of your plan?




What should be done to reduce the likelihood of the problems, or at least minimize the effect should they occur?

# Index

Advertising investment, 2
Air conditioning system, 38
Audience considerations, 75, 77, 78

Benefits analysis, 59–70
Brainstorming technique:
    appropriate use of, 9, 50
    courses of action, 51
    logical approach to, 51
    tape recording, 51
    visual record, 50
Budgeted expenses reduction, 56

Capital requirement, 67
Child development, 49
Choice of action (*see* Factors influencing choice of action)
Communications skills, 74
Complaints from customers, 4
Compromise:
    arriving at, 56
    need for, 55
Confidence:
    in decision making, 12, 69
    in recommendation presentation, 76
Consultation, need for wider, 1
Creative thinking:
    discouraging, 48
    need for, 48
    vs logical thinking, 48
Creativity:
    development, 50
    discouraging, 50, 52
Customer incentives, 2
Customer satisfaction, 55

Decision making:
    adverse effects of, 2–3
    attitudes towards, 3–4
    confidence in, 12, 69
    definition, 5
    dithering in, 5
    domestic, 6–7
    factors influencing, 8
    improving your skills, 83
    knock-on effect, 7
    putting into practice, 83–96
    right or wrong, 6, 7
    steps in, 8–12
    time needed for, 5
    too quick, 6
    (*see also* Factors influencing choice of action; Objective clarification)
Decision Making Organization (*see* DM Organization)

# INDEX

Decisiveness:
  definition, 5
  examples of, 5–6
Design improvement, 21
Disabled persons, provision for, 38
Dithering in decision making, 5
DM Organization case study, 22–34
  background to, 22
  clarifying the objective, 32–34
  comparison of options, 57–69
  design and development director's report, 32
  finance director's report, 27, 32
  financial situation, 24–25
  future direction, 26–31
  layout of, 23
  list of options, 52–53
  manufacturing director's report, 27–28, 32
  personnel director's report, 30, 33
  plant and facilities director's report, 30, 33
  present situation, 26
  product design director's report, 29
  safety aspects, 31
  sales director's report, 28, 32
  space problem, 40–46, 57–59
  staff turnover, 31
  training programme, 31
Domestic decision making, 6–7

Economic factors, 55
Efficiency improvement, 56
Emotional control, 49
Emotional feelings, 49
Equipment decisions, 47
Essential factors (*see* Factors influencing choice of action; Options)
Essential services, 1
Expenditure requests, 71–72
Expenses cutback, 55

Factors influencing choice of action, 35–46, 85
  check list, 46
  DM Organization case study, 40
  'essential', 43, 46
  example of importance of, 35
  extending into specific statements, 41, 46, 85
  guidelines for development of, 45–46
  house purchase example, 39
  identifying those of maximum value, 43–44
  minimizing time involved, 42
  sample specification, 44–45
  space problems, 40–46
  top priorities, 44, 46
Factory closure effects, 37
Fear in discouraging objectivity, 52
Feelings, 68

House purchase factors, 39
Human factors, 55, 67

Implementation plan, 10–12, 79–81
  assigning responsibilities in, 80
  guidelines for, 80–81
  monitoring, 81
  potential problems, 81
  sequence of events, 80
  setting out, 95
  target dates, 80
Incentives to new customers, 2
Industrial relations, 37
Information:
  collection of, 8, 59
  effective use of, 9
  inquisitive desire for, 49
  need to establish requirements, 15
  need for, 6
  need for provision of, 15

# INDEX

Information—*continued*
  prior need for, 4
  sharing technological, 73
  validity of, 5–6, 64
Information presentation:
  skills required in, 74
  successful, 74
  unsuccessful, 73
  (*see also* Recommendation presentation)
Information recording, 60
Insurance costs, 56
Investment:
  advertising, 2
  essential areas, 1
  research and development, 2
  sales, 2
  training, 2

Leadership powers, 37
Location decisions, 47
Logical approach to brainstorming, 51
Logical thinking vs creative thinking, 48
Lost business, 5

Maintenance aspects, 56
Manpower decisions, 47
Manufacturing capability, overstretched, 4
Manufacturing costs, 56
Manufacturing problems, sales team's knowledge of, 14
Matrix methods, 59–61, 66, 88, 90
Monitoring systems, 81
Morale aspects, 55

Need for improvement, 1–12
  example of, 1
New business, encouraging, 2
New ideas, generating, 48

Objective clarification, 8, 13–34
  as logical progression to effectively implemented decision, 18
  case study, 19–22
  confusion in, 16
  DM Organization case study, 32–34
  examples of need for, 13–14
  guidelines for, 17
  in recommendation presentation, 74–75
  need to concentrate on, 20–21
  statement on, 34, 84
Objectivity, fear factor in, 52
Options:
  all-round implications of, 10
  choice of, 9, 42, 55
    guidelines for, 69–70
  comparison of, 8, 9, 55–70, 90
    against essential factors, 88
    DM Organization case study, 57–69
    guidelines for, 69–70
    symbols for, 60
  conflicting issues, 55
  eliminating, 9, 56, 68
  essential factors, 56, 57, 59, 64, 88
  generating, 9, 21, 47–53
    DM Organization case study, 52–53
    (*see also* Brainstorming; Creative thinking; Creativity)
  identifying, 9
  shortlisting, 42
  status quo, 9, 51
Order processing department, 37–38

Personal prejudice, 9
Pessimism, constructive, 64
Planning skills, 80
Powers of leadership, 37
Price increases, extreme, 3

# INDEX

Product knowledge, increasing, 15
Profitability improvement, 18, 20, 21
Project request form, 72
Project systems, 72
Purchasing decisions, 18

Quality improvement, 56

Raw material stock turnover, 33–34
Recession:
 as scapegoat, 3
 effects of, 1, 2
Recommendation presentation, 71–78
 closure, 78
 confidence in, 76
 content of, 75
 example of failure, 73
 framework for, 75, 78, 93
 guidelines for, 77–78
 method of, 10
 notes use during, 76
 potential problems, 96
 practice, 76
 preparation need, 92
 prerequisites for success, 76
 rules of preparation, 74–76
 venue and facilities, 76
 visual aids, 75
 (*see also* Information presentation)
Recruitment decisions, 16–17
Research and development
  investment, 2
Responsibility for action, 79–80
Responsibility overlapping, 80
Reward for efforts, 16

Risk analysis, 59–70
Risk areas, 66
Risk elements, 55

Safety aspects, 31, 38
Safety records, 56
Sales budget increase, 73
Sales investment, 2
Sales promotions, 4
Sales team, knowledge of manufacturing problems, 14
Scapegoats in the event of failure, 3
Security controls, 71–72
Service decisions, 47
Smoking restrictions, 56
Space problem, 5, 33, 34, 40–46, 57–59
Staff turnover, 31
Status differences, 38
Status quo as option, 9, 51

Tape recorder in brainstorming, 51
Time saving, 42
Training courses, 16
Training investment, 2
Training programme, 31

Visual aids in recommendation presentation, 75
Visual record in brainstorming, 50

Wage differentials, 37
Water meter case study, 19–22
 sample objectives, 20
Weighbridge security control, 71–72